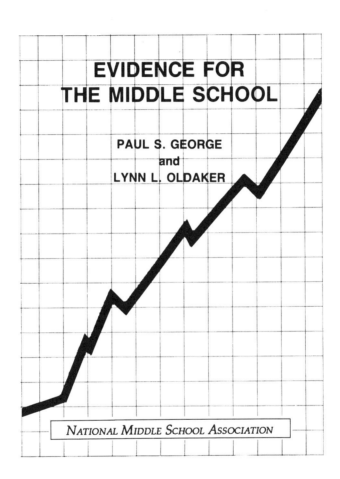

EVIDENCE FOR
THE MIDDLE SCHOOL

PAUL S. GEORGE
and
LYNN L. OLDAKER

NATIONAL MIDDLE SCHOOL ASSOCIATION

i

NATIONAL MIDDLE SCHOOL ASSOCIATION

Paul George, Professor of Education at the University of Florida in Gainesville, is one of the nation's leading proponents of the middle school. A prolific and able writer as well as a widely traveled consultant and speaker, Dr. George's impact on the movement has been substantial.

Lynn Oldaker, although a native of Georgia, has resided in Juneau, Alaska for eight years where she is a middle school teacher. Active in the National Middle School Association, Ms. Oldaker spent the 1983-84 year studying middle school education at the University of Florida.

Copyright © 1985 by National Middle School Association
4807 Evanswood Dr., Columbus, OH 43229-6292
Fourth Printing, January 1992

ISBN 1-56090-026-1

Printed by Baesman Printing Corporation, 2120 Hardy Parkway, Cols., OH 43223

Contents

FOREWORD

"Evidence for the Middle School." The title itself excites. How eagerly have educators caught up in this major educational movement sought just this. And while this monograph is certainly not the last word, and the authors carefully make no such claim, it is an important and an encouraging word for certain. This publication begins to fill the frequently noted research void in the middle school movement. There has been a tremendous, enthusiastic, and often impassioned voice promoting middle schools in the last twenty years. That advocacy, however, has often been turned aside because of the unavailability of sufficient evidence to validate the practices proposed. A gut-level certainty that they were on sound ground sustained the already converted advocates, but it didn't always convince board of education members and others.

The failure of traditional educational research to influence practice at any school level has been a concern of educators for many years. Typically, experimental research studies have been too narrow in their focus, have had too few numbers involved, and covered too brief a time to yield adequate results. The complexities of classroom environments and the myriad factors which exert influence on the on-going instructional process have made it all but impossible to conduct experimental studies the results of which could become operative in classroom teaching on any widespread scale.

On the other hand, general status studies which sought to compare middle schools with junior high schools were usually equally ineffective. These survey studies seldom touched the real programmatic factors, assumed differences based on school title or grade organization, and, not surprisingly, produced inconclusive and disappointing results.

To change classroom and school practices, then, it was evident that a different type of educational research was needed. Such an approach has emerged and is having an impact on middle school education.

In the first section of this timely publication, Paul George reviews research activities in middle level education and describes this new research thrust. He then details the results which a number of studies employing this newer type research in middle level schools have produced. These studies have yielded substantial evidence to support the efficacy of the middle school concept.

In Part Two, Paul George and Lynn Oldaker report on the extensive study they conducted of 130 middle schools which had been deemed particularly successful or exemplary. These schools rather uniformly evidenced a number of common characteristics, the very characteristics which have received consensus endorsement as central to the middle school concept. While the authors are cautious in generalizing and guard against overstating, the results, nevertheless, are very encouraging. Middle level schools that have been judged by others as outstanding display a consistent and almost universal incidence of team organization, teacher-based guidance activities, flexible use of time, faculty participation in decision making, and other tenets of the middle school concept. And they report highly positive results in academic achievement, school climate, faculty morale, student behavior and other factors. This is evidence for the middle school! And those of us who are committed to middle level education now have additional ''scripture'' to support our advocacy. It behooves us to become familiar with the contents of this monograph and help spread the good news.

John H. Lounsbury
Editor, NMSA Publications

Part I

Research In Middle Level Education

A BRIEF REVIEW OF RESEARCH ACTIVITIES

The middle school movement is one of the largest and most comprehensive efforts at educational reorganization in the history of American public schooling. Hundreds of school districts, now perhaps thousands, in all fifty states, have moved toward the middle school plan, and the reorganization to middle schools, it appears, will continue unabated into the remaining years of the twentieth century. Each year, dozens of school districts open newly reorganized middle schools as alternatives to K-8, 7-9, 7-12, or other pre-existing plans. In spite of a decline in the overall number of all types of schools in America as a result of decreasing enrollments, the number of identified middle schools continues to increase (NIE, 1983).

New efforts in the reorganization of middle level education are not restricted to the United States. Dozens of middle schools are now available to students in Canada, the United Kingdom, and in many international schools in Europe, South American and Asia. Japan has become increasingly dissatisfied with the junior high school program and at least one Japanese educational expert has spent a full year studying middle schools in the United States. China also offers what are called middle schools. Early adolescent education is an increasingly international concern.

Until recently, research reports on the effectiveness of middle school education have been inconclusive; confusing language and research design difficulties have introduced a considerable degree of misunderstanding into the discussions of middle school effectiveness at local, state, and national levels. Often, middle schools in name only have been compared with other middle level organizations, with the predictable lack of significant results as the outcome of dozens of studies. Consequently, educators, policymakers, and citizens are left without sufficient reliable information about whether such schools work better than the school organizations they replaced.

1

Beginning in the mid-sixties, middle schools often appear in many districts as an educational expediency resulting from court-ordered desegregation, declining enrollments, or some other need not exclusively related to the education of young adolescents. For almost two decades, therefore, middle schools lacked adequate definition. Only in the last several years have educators begun to arrive at any relatively complete consensus on the characteristics of successful middle schools. More recently, many educators with experience in middle level schools for older children and young adolescents strongly suggest some common elements: classroom-based guidance efforts; organizing teachers into interdisciplinary teams responsible for the same group of children; arrangements which permit the development of longer-term relationships between teachers and the students they teach; an enriched curriculum; flexible use of time; instructional strategies that consider the characteristics of the learner; a wide range of exploratory experiences keyed to the interests of middle school youth; and collaboration between and among teachers and administrators as they work to improve middle school programs (Alexander and George, 1981). There is evidence to suggest that such program components are finding their way into more and more middle schools regardless of the name of the school or the grade levels included (McEwin and Clay, 1983); yet there is, to date, unfortunately, too little evidence on the effectiveness of such components in middle level schools.

This situation is distressingly ironic. The middle school movement is more than a quarter of a century old, and of such magnitude that it is unequalled by any other national educational effort, save the century-long school consolidation movement, yet articles asking whether the middle school is a fad continue to generate widespread interest and concern (Klingele, 1985). School administrators, curriculum planners, university professors, parents and bureaucrats at all levels profess ignorance of the basic components of the middle school. Even educators involved in so-called middle schools sometimes lack knowledge of the differences between the middle school and other school plans serving young adolescents. Although such issues were resolved years ago, some continue to ask whether the grade levels included in the middle school, or the name of the school, make a difference in the outcomes for students. There are 20 million students being educated in today's American middle level schools and massive changes in these schools have been occurring for almost three decades, leaving virtually no American untouched. Until recently, however, there has been very little research support, or criticism, for particular approaches to the the education of these children and youth (Johnston, 1984).

School board members and parent groups considering new middle school programs often seek evidence that will support their reorganization effort, and turn to those with experience in middle schools. But, unfortunately, experienced middle school members are often in the difficult and embarrassing position of being unable to compile research support for the program that they feel so strongly about and that they know, from personal experience, has been tremendously successful.

Why the lack of research support? Is it because there have been no improvements, no progress, not even any differences? Are the thousands of educators, parents, and students who are extremely positive about middle school programs merely victims of the Hawthorne or halo effect? Would any change have worked as well as the new middle school programs? Worse, was their success imaginary or fabricated?

The answers to these questions are important. No patron or policy maker should be expected to embrace a reorganization plan requiring massive resource shifts, considerable dislocation of teachers and students, and expensive training programs without asking for some concrete evidence that the effort is likely to be worth it. No one should be discouraged from asking these difficult questions, even though the answers are even more difficult to develop. Our social tradition insists that the burden of the proof is upon those who advocate the changes, not those who ask the questions.

It is not as if this is the first time major innovations have occurred in American education without any research support. In fact, as most educators know, the history of innovation and change in our schools is replete with instances of changes which came about, on a major scale, for every reason except that there was research evidence available for whatever was proposed. One example should be sufficient.

About twenty years ago, the first open space school buildings made their appearance. In a very short time, hundreds of new open space schools were designed, constructed, and opened all across the land. In an equally short time, teachers and parents reacted extremely negatively; soon portable walls were erected, followed by permanent walls in a year or two. Twenty years later, there are almost no open space schools being built and the once wide-open spaces are nothing more than cramped versions of traditional classrooms.

After all of this, what do we know about the effectiveness of open space schools? What did research tell us? Virtually nothing. After reviewing almost 200 research studies of open space schools, one reviewer concluded that most of the research was so flawed that we learned nothing from it (George, 1975).

The predominant pattern of research on open space schools was, of course, a comparison of open space schools with traditional school buildings, and the predominant result was a report of no significant differences. It is likely that most open space schools never really operated as they were intended; individualized instruction and real team teaching did not appear the way designers had planned. Many open space schools ended up, therefore, containing exactly the same style of instruction, grouping and self-contained classes that were present in the traditional schools. Hence, many research studies compared two building designs that housed the same type of programs, with the expected results, no significant difference.

It might be argued that the open space school phenomenon was a fad that lasted about twenty years, touched many districts, affected the lives of many students and then faded away. The reasonable extension of that argument to the middle school, for some, might lead to a prediction of a similar end for the middle school movement. This is, happily, unlikely to occur.

A NEW RESEARCH STRATEGY: THE OUTLIER STUDY

Fortunately for the middle school, and for the advocates of that program, the middle school movement has emerged during a propitious period in the history of educational research. In the last twenty years, great progress has been made in the conduct of educational research; a point of maturity has been reached. Instead of making specious comparisons of subjects that cannot be reasonably compared, or conducting experiments in situations where experimental research has no place, researchers have developed a new degree of skill in seeking the answers to important questions. It appears that this new sophistication in social science research emerged at just about the same time as the middle school was born, about a quarter of a century ago.

Almost 20 years ago, James Coleman (1966) published a national study that focused on equal educational opportunity. After amassing mountains of data about student achievement, this influential study concluded that the only really significant factor in academic achievement was the socioeconomic status of the children who attended a school. The "home effect", as it came to be called, appeared to outweigh anything that educators attempted to do, and the implication was that teachers did not matter, that schools made no difference in the lives of the students who attended. Race and socioeconomic status were, it was implied, the determining factors in academic achievement; the "school effect" was unimportant and inconsequential.

Charges that teachers were inconsequential and that schools made no difference in the lives of children were, to educators, almost as infuriating as the implication that the children of the poor could not learn. Twenty years later, landmark research in what has come to be called "teacher and school effectiveness" is being eagerly consumed in virtually every school district and college of education in the country. This effectiveness research has demonstrated, quite clearly, that teachers do make a difference and that poor children can learn well. Major efforts at school improvement, based on this research, are underway in hundreds of districts and student achievement scores are responding positively.

Interestingly, at almost the same time, researchers in the corporate and industrial sector were pursuing a similar pathway. Staggering beneath the blows from competition from European and Asian companies, American corporate economists attempted to find a formula that worked. As it turned out, researchers from these two very different areas, education and corporate life, reached their breakthrough points using the same research process.

In education, as in industry, these successful efforts came to be known among researchers as "outlier studies." The term "outlier study" refers to research focused on the careful scrutiny of the most successful examples of a subject that could be found, those that lay outside the boundaries of the mediocre. Outlier studies concentrate on attempting to learn what makes the best become the best. In corporate life, the outlier research focused on corporations that managed to remain highly productive and profitable over long periods of time (Peters and Waterman, 1982). In education, it became the search for and study of the most successful teachers and the barrier-breaking schools.

In education, this research followed several basic steps. First, researchers rejected the claim that there are no differences between teachers or schools. They began with the assumption that teachers can make a difference and that schools do matter. Second, they sought examples of teachers and schools who could be demonstrated to have made significant differences in the lives of students; they identified classrooms and schools where students make gains that went far beyond what could have been predicted or expected. Third, these exceptional teachers and schools became points of discovery, not of experiment. That is, researchers went to the classrooms and the schools where the successes were documented and attempted to discover what made the difference. Fourth, having discovered and described the characteristics of effectiveness in separate classrooms and schools, researchers then compared what they discovered about successful teachers to see what they might have in common. They examined the characteristics of successful schools to learn whether such schools have important similarities that could be linked to improved academic achievement. Finally, the researchers have attempted to develop models that can be used in assisting other teachers and schools to become more successful.

Instead of pursuing laboratory experiments, recent educational researchers have gone into the field to discover what works well. Theory emerged from the discoveries, not the reverse. As a result, educators are now much more able to identify which teacher behaviors are likely to be correlated with increased academic achievement and which characteristics of successful schools are common among the schools that make really positive differences in the lives of their students. While much more must be learned about such teachers and schools, and even these conclusions must be accepted only tentatively, it is reasonable to expect that continued efforts in these areas will be likely to produce additional useful insights. Summaries of the results of the research on teacher and school effectiveness are available in a number of sources (George, 1983).

In the last five years, the pursuit of outlier studies as measures of school effectiveness has been extended into the area of middle school education, and while that effort is in its infancy, the same positive results have begun to appear. Based on the assumption that schools do make a difference in the lives of their students, and that the degree and type of differences can be traced to the characteristics of the schools in question, educational researchers have uncovered some important findings. While it may be premature to claim that answers to all the hard questions have been developed, it does appear that certain very important trends or themes can be noted and discussed.

RECENT RESEARCH FINDINGS

Following the general guidelines for the new research strategy, a number of different researchers, in quite different settings and for very different purposes, have pursued their studies in quite similar fashion. Accepting the argument that grade level and name of the school are unlikely to be the cause for any significant differences among schools, oversimplified and specious comparisons of middle and junior high schools have not been the focus. Nor has any time been wasted on further futile attempts to determine which combination of grade levels holds the secret to success with early adolescents. Those days, one hopes, are over.

Recent research has, instead, focused on the identification of schools that have an outstanding record of success which can be demonstrated to be free of dependence on the socioeconomic status or ethnic backgrounds of the students attending the school. Typically, an outstanding record of success is established by determining that the schools measure up to a number of important criteria for success (Lipsitz, 1984; Rutter, 1979).

These factors include academic achievement scores on standarized tests, attendance rates, behavior in school, behavior out of school (i.e., delinquency), parental satisfaction, and reputations for excellence at the local, state, or even the national level. Once these criteria had been satisfied, the schools became the subjects of intensive indepth investigation.

One of the first such studies was conducted by Rutter and his associates (1979) in twelve junior high schools in inner-city London. Since the study was published, it has become extremely well-known and is discussed in detail in almost all of the reports of research on school effectiveness. It is significant for persons interested in middle level education because of the rigor of the research design and the fact that the findings provide an exciting confirmation of some of the central components of the middle school concept, in spite of the fact that they were discovered in junior high school settings.

Rutter discovered that within this sample of twelve junior high schools, several of the schools were very successful while others were not. Successful outcomes were not a matter of grade level or school name, obviously, since all twelve schools had the same name and grade levels. Nor were the successful schools identified by their physical or administrative features, the socio-economic background of the students, or the differences in the elementary schools which fed the junior highs. The reasons for the success of some of the schools and the failure of others in this study appear to be related to two different but closely related sets of factors: academic emphasis and the psychosocial environment.

As has been the case, generally, in the area of research on teacher and school effectiveness, the Rutter study confirms the importance of an academic emphasis. Reasonably high expectations, direct instruction, homework, and other related items combine to enable teachers and students to take learning seriously and, as a result, to become more successful in mastering the learning tasks. In addition to this academic emphasis, however, Rutter and his colleagues concluded that the really crucial differences between the successful and unsuccessful schools in the study were in the area of the psychosocial environment, in the life of the school as a social organization.

A positive psychosocial environment is the enabling force which permits teachers to be successful with the academic emphasis in the first place. The academically successful schools were those where the teachers and the students were able to see themselves as part of the same group, as members of the same team. Teachers and students, in the schools that reached beyond the expectations or predicted levels of achievement and behavior, shared the same educational perspective, the same norms for the life of the school.

Most important, insofar as the middle school is concerned, is that all of the factors that led to the "ethos of caring" characteristic of the successful schools are part and parcel of today's American middle school concept. Teachers working together, planning jointly, to establish conditions for students, promoting increased responsibilities and participation of students, establishing stable teaching and friendship groups that last for more than one year — all of these factors lay close to the heart of the middle school movement. Rutter understood, and makes clear, the insignificance of the concerns for the name of the school, the grade levels included, or other factors which have been mistakenly perceived as important to the middle school by those new or uniformed about the process of middle level education (George, 1983, 71):

> Rutter concluded, after four years of study, that the crucial differences in the schools boiled down to whether or not the school effectively attended to the social side of learning. It is critically important, says Rutter, that teachers and students come to see themselves as part of the same school group, the same team. This unity permits faculty and students to work together for common purposes in and outside the classroom. Unity is what makes it more likely that students will share the educational perspective of the faculty, and what, therefore, leads ultimately to higher academic achievement.

Not too long after the Rutter study became known, Phi Delta Kappa published its own outlier study of the characteristics of schools that had what that association called *good discipline.* Over 500 schools responded to a detailed questionnaire that helped to establish the common characteristics of schools known for good student behavior. Among the recommendations that emerged from the study were several that middle school advocates would claim as central to that approach to the education of early adolescents (Phi Delta Kappa, 1982):

> Schools should find ways to improve how people in the school work together to solve problems.
> Schools should develop the means to reduce authority and status differences among all persons in the school.
> Schools should increase and widen the students' sense of belonging in the school.
> Schools should find a way to deal with the personal problems that affect life within the school. Programs called "advisor-advisee" were advocated.
> Schools should improve the physical and organizational arrangements so that these factors reinforce other efforts.

The writer, at least, finds it very easy to see in the above studies a clear, if unannounced, reference to organizational approaches of the middle school such as the interdisciplinary team, the advisory program, and arrangements such as multiage grouping that permit strongly positive relationships, once established, to endure for more than one academic year. It appears that distinctions which sharply separated concepts of curriculum and instruction from those of school organization are now obsolete; school organization is as much a part of the curriculum as the courses of study presented to students.

Further support for this perspective on the centrality of school organization to the middle school concept emerged that same year in an important study at the University of Florida (Damico, 1982). A group of social psychologists and sociologists, concerned about how middle school organization might affect interracial contact among early adolescents, examined student interaction in six different middle level schools in the same school district. The schools had the same grade levels, the same designation (middle) and were attended by students from similar ethnic and socioeconomic backgrounds. The curriculum was the same in each school, established by curriculum committees and identical textbooks at the school district level. Everything about the schools was as similar as it could be, except for the ways in which the schools were organized.

Two of the six schools were organized as the middle school concept suggests, with interdisciplinary team organization, advisory groups, and multiage grouping which permitted teachers and students to stay together on the same team for three years. The other four schools had academic departments without teams, no advisory program and were organized so that teachers and students changed every academic year, with students being reorganized into new class groups each year. Because advisory programs and multiage grouping are, in several ways, components of the team organization, the real difference between the two groups of schools was that two schools had complete, fully-functioning teams and the others had no team organization at all.

Researchers concluded, after extensive examination of the interracial interaction in the schools, that the schools with the interdisciplinary team organization had a much more positive interracial climate. Students in these teamed schools had far more cross-race interactions, and these interactions resulted in significantly more positive perceptions of students of other races. Black students in the teamed schools saw school as being significantly better than did black students in the non-teamed schools. Students in teamed schools had more friends of other races and reported that the school was better and friendlier. Even in situations that could be observed, such as seating in the cafeteria and assemblies, there was much more voluntary cross racial seating. In the teamed schools, white students evaluated black students more positively, perceived interracial classroom climates more positively, and believed that interracial relationships, in general, were more positive than did white students in the non-teamed schools. It seems clear that the team organization, with the advisory group program and multiage grouping, contributes significantly to the improvement of race relationships among young adolescents.

As an extension of this study of student perspectives of interracial relationships, Doda (1984) pursued an ethnographic analysis of two of the schools, one with the middle school concept, one without. Observing and analyzing several teachers in each of the two schools throughout the length of a school year, Doda discovered that teachers' perspectives and practices were "markedly different and that these differences were associated with the organization, curriculum and administration of the two schools" (Doda, vi).

At the middle school, teachers saw their role as an exalted one, difficult but terribly important. At the other school, however, teachers lacked these convictions, tending to view teaching as a burdened semi-profession with little opportunity to shape students' lives or futures. At the middle school, teachers saw themselves as responsible for helping students in a multitude of ways, whereas teachers at the second school saw themselves almost exclusively as disseminators of subject matter. These disparate goals and priorities found expression in the manner and style of classroom instruction and management.

While it would be premature to attempt to assign causality, it seems equally unwise to assume that school organization had no affect on teacher perspective or behavior. Doda argues that the team organization prompted a different perspective on the part of the middle school teachers she studied. These teachers valued each other, looked to one another for support and assistance, and talked of the educational process as a collective effort. At the other school, where no team organization existed, the teachers had significantly less contact with one another, and the contact that did occur was often brief and rarely task-related. In an earlier description of this activity, Doda described it this way (1982, 10):

Life as a team member contributes to the middle school teacher's world view. It provides frequent teacher contact, opportunities to discuss the students that teachers have in common and it allows experimentation and the testing of new ideas. The team provides its teachers with comradery, support and friendship. Teachers view themselves as part of a collective which mitigates the burden of individual failure while bolstering professional self-esteem. Perhaps most important, the team is a decision-making unit. Teachers must make decisions collectively and must continually share ideas, attitudes, beliefs, views and feelings. It may be this continual dialogue among teachers that promotes the teachers' view that their work is significant. Moreover, the challenge of joint decision-making may provide a sense of power and control not found in the isolated teaching experience typical in the junior high school.

Working in the junior high's structure provided little of no opportunity for comradery or affiliation with a collective identity. Teachers spent most of their time alone and shared very few dimensions of school life with fellow colleagues. The burden of failure was largely an individual matter. The range of decisions made by the department was limited to that of curriculum and teachers generally did not discuss beliefs and ideas at length. The department serviced efficiency and did not encourage teacher interaction. Moreover, the department was not seen as a unit involved in school decision-making. While department chairpersons did meet from time to time with the administration, those meetings did not deal with school philosophy and policy. The department chairpersons were spokespersons for the department's curriculum concerns and there was seldom an opportunity for discussion of other school matters. Department membership did not require extensive involvement and participation. What teachers held in common was the curriculum and individuals could execute the same curriculum with little dialogue between fellow members. The tasks they performed could best be done alone. This may account for the individualistic orientation that prevails at the junior high and perhaps simultaneously reinforces the focus on procedures over people.

One of the least known features of some exemplary middle schools, multiage grouping, permits teachers and students to stay together on the same team for more than one year. In her study, Doda identified this feature as having particular significance in its impact on teacher perspectives and practices (1982, 13-14):

Contrasting teacher emphases on students in the middle school and curriculum in the junior high may be more related to multiage grouping than to any other single difference. At the middle school teachers had the same students for three years. They viewed the three year experience as the most satisfying part of their job because it allowed them to see students grow and change over time. In three years, growth is generally dramatic in all areas of development. Perhaps teachers have a better chance of feeling exalted about their work and maintaining their focus on student development when they teach youngsters for an extended time and can witness this dramatic growth. For the teachers at the junior high who only have students for one year, student and teacher achievement are less obvious. Teachers' focus on short term results in curriculum mastery and test grades. Chances are that the teachers only glean that sense of heroic pride when a student returns years later for a visit. The entire staff at the middle school took an interest in making school enjoyable for students, while the staff at the junior high did not. No doubt, teachers' notions of students' improvability account for this, in part. However, the multiage grouping and teacher-student guidance program in the middle school resulted in teachers spending more time with students outside of the classroom. This produced a focus on teacher-student relationships and in those relationships teachers were faced with students' honest feelings about school and learning. Recognition that school wasn't much fun for most students seemed to be a part of teachers' concerted efforts to make it otherwise. The indifference of teachers in the junior high regarding their responsibility for generating student enthusiasm could be explained by their infrequent opportunities to schedule fun into the school day. There were very few times during a school year when classes were suspended for a special student event. This was not so at the middle school. In addition, teachers did not have as much contact with students in a non-academic setting. The teacher-student relationships were preempted by academic demands, grades, and changing bells. Teachers may have been able to avoid the real concerns and feelings of their students. This difference in orientation could be due in part to teachers' role perception and their focus towards learning. Can and should learning be fun? The junior high teachers did not seem to recognize themselves as motivators — motivating students was not a deeply felt role.

During this same period, researchers at the Center for Early Adolescence, in Carrboro, North Carolina, undertook a study of schools which had been identified, according to their criteria, as being particularly responsive to the developmental needs of young adolescents (Dorman, 1983; Lipsitz, 1984). Selecting from among many that were nominated, the researchers identified four schools to be observed in great depth. At the end of the intensive observations, the researchers concluded that, while there was no single model that could be prescribed exclusively, there were common themes present in each of the four highly successful schools. Lipsitz (1984,

167) describes the most striking of these common features as the schools' "willingness and ability to adapt all school practices to the individual differences in intellectual, biological and social maturation of their students." The schools set out to establish a positive learning climate, not just because it would lead to increased academic achievement, but because it was something which possessed intrinsic value in the education of young adolescents.

These middle schools were successful because they built their programs on an understanding of and a commitment to the characteristics of early adolescents as learners and human beings. To respond positively to these students, all of the four schools stressed the fact that they were not secondary schools based on a junior or high school model.

Each school used an organizational strategy that helped develop a sense of community in a group small enough for early adolescents to feel real membership; each school produced smallness within bigness. While none of the four schools had the exact same method or organizing students, all had a house or team structure, some of which were organized so that multiage grouping permitted the teachers and students to experience the long term relationships which other researchers have begun to identify as significant. As Lipsitz (1984, 194) expresses it, the team or house:

> minimizes size, personalizes the environment, increases communication among students and teachers, and reduces tension. The schools have all reduced the influence of subject-oriented departments in order to empower multidisciplinary teams. They have guaranteed teachers common planning periods so that every student is known predictably by a team of teachers who have time to consult with one another about his or her academic progress and general well-being. The common planning period also promotes collegiality and professionalism in curriculum development and review.

Reinforcing the conclusions that Doda reached about the effect of the team organization on teacher perspectives, Lipsitz observed that the "psychic rewards for teaching in these schools are high," and that there is a highly unusual lack of adult isolation in the schools (Lipsitz, 186-7):

> Common planning and lunch periods, team meetings, and team teaching encourage constant communication and allow for high levels of companionship. Teachers are not abandoned to their students, which is very important in working with the age group, with which daily experiences may not necessarily be rewarding.

In an earlier summary of the research, Lipsitz (n.d., 6) concluded:

> Finally, while it is not possible to say how widespread excellence in middle-grade schooling is, we can conclude from these four schools

13

that young adolescents and adults can live and learn together in peaceable school communities; that dichotomies like quality vs. equity and academic vs. social goals need not be mutually exclusive; and that with diverse means and in diverse circumstances, middle schools can be breeding grounds for academic excellence and social development.

A recent outlier-style examination of the characteristics of effective inner-city intermediate schools (Levine, 1984) contained descriptions of schools in Watts, Brooklyn, the Bronx, and Detroit. These schools, with demonstrably higher academic achievement than others in the same situations, were found to have undergone "significant structural change" on the way to improvement. Organizational arrangements which created a more personal environment, or in Rutter's language, an "ethos of caring", were high on the list of effective innovations. Team organization which facilitated group planning and students' personal growth were at the heart of the improvement process. Levine (p. 711) and his colleagues concluded:

> We believe that significant structural change is a requirement for effective instruction at inner-city secondary schools; efforts to improve teaching methods at inner-city junior...high schools are not likely to have much impact unless accompanied by appropriate structural changes in instructional and organizational arrangements.

It is difficult to examine this current research in the education of young adolescents and not realize how unimportant concerns like the name of the school or the grade levels are to the outcomes of students. Furthermore, it seems clear that another reason much of the research has been fruitless is the false assumption that the middle school reorganization process has been, primarily, one of change in the curriculum offered to the students or of new instructional strategies to present the materials to be learned.

There is little evidence for the view that changes in curriculum and instruction have been central to the middle school movement. Much of what students learn in the eighth grade is the same regardless of the school in which they learn it. The curriculum and instruction students experience is probably what their parents also experienced, or endured. While it may be accurate to argue that changes in the curriculum and instructional program of schools for early adolescents should have come first, this has apparently not been the case. Perhaps the attempts to change the curriculum that did occur where short-lived because, as Levine writes, they were too often implemented without important corresponding changes in the organization of the school.

The most recent research in middle level education suggests that organizational restructuring is, however, happening in an increasingly larger number of schools, and that this reorganization is very similar, even though it occurs in very diverse school settings and in very diverse communities. Furthermore, the research has begun to suggest that these efforts at reorganization do, indeed, promote higher academic achievement and improve personal development for the youth who are fortunate enough to experience such a program.

Part II

A Survey of the Effectiveness of Middle Level Schools

THE DESIGN OF THE STUDY

The present study was designed to gather evidence regarding the effectiveness of contemporary middle school education in the United States. In particular, two areas were investigated: 1) the extent to which middle schools identified as exemplary contain program components which conform to the recommendations of the literature on middle school education, and 2) the outcomes of such programs. Central office staff members and school administrators in 34 states, involving 160 schools, were invited to supply evidence about the existence of certain programs and of the positive and negative effects of the implementation of middle school programs in their districts.

A list of reputedly exemplary middle schools was developed from middle schools identified by 1) the 1982 Study of Well-disciplined Schools sponsored by Phi Delta Kappa, 2) the 1983 U.S.D.O.E. National Secondary School Recognition Program, 3) a panel of ten persons recognized as experts in middle school education, and 4) several lists of exemplary schools identified in recent books on middle school education. Of this number, 130 schools responded, yielding a return rate of 81%.

In October and November 1983, each participant received a letter requesting assistance in the collection of evidence regarding the effects of implementing middle schools in each system. Respondents were asked to complete a lengthy questionnaire providing details on the date of reorganization, the nature of the middle school program being offered, the size of the school, and other factors indicating the extent to which the school included the characteristics of an exemplary program. Each was also asked to estimate the effects of reorganization on 38 different factors in ten categories. Finally, respondents were asked to provide more concrete factual evidence of the effects of middle school programs on student achievement, discipline, personal development, faculty morale, and school spirit. Many respondents supplied the results of formal school evaluations in their districts, annual reports of school progress, photographs, and other data relating to the outcomes of school reorganization.[1]

Limitations and Assumptions

The findings of this study apply most directly to middle schools which contain the components referred to in the description of the sample which follows. No attempt was made to control or to analyze data on the basis of socioeconomic status, school size, geographic location, or the influence of school leadership or talented instruction.

The study is also limited by the fact that respondents were encouraged to supply evidence regarding the positive effects of middle school education in their districts. Negative data, while sought, were not as strenuously pursued. It is possible, therefore, that as a consequence of the design of the study, the few persons who failed to respond may have done so because they had fewer positive experiences to relate, and that those who did respond may have elected to exclude negative data.

---

[1]Persons interested in the details of the study may write to Dr. George.

REPRESENTATIONS OF THE
EXEMPLARY MIDDLE SCHOOL

One important outcome of the present study was the discovery of the striking similarity in the components of the exemplary middle schools included in the study. Like the earlier research of Lipsitz, Levine and others, these data indicate that effective schools manifest markedly similar programs, regardless of the diversity of their locations or other distinguishing features. The programmatic congruence of schools thought to be highly successful is, in fact, astounding.

Interdisciplinary team organization is a central feature of 90% of the schools in the study. Common groups of students taught by an interdisciplinary team of teachers who are located closely together and who have common planning periods is the rule in the schools in this study. Team planning in these schools results in common rules and procedures, parent and student conferences, and other collaborative efforts. Teachers and students are involved, in dozens of these school sites, in the creation of a spirit, a sense of community, that is clearly linked to the "ethos of caring" referred to by Rutter (1979). Collaborative efforts extend, occasionally at least, to instruction. More often, teachers engage in a participatory decision-making that marked the effective inner-city schools studied by Levine (1984).

While an even larger percentage of schools (94%) provided for a flexibly scheduled school day that permitted teams of teachers to modify their programs as they believed wise, 93% included a home-base, advisor-advisee program for each child. In spite of the fact that middle school educators appear to have been, to date, unable to find a magically successful formula for the advisory program, exemplary schools persist in experimenting and insist on continuing an effort of this sort. It reflects the intense commitment of these educators to adapt the program to the child, rather than the reverse. In fact, 99% of the respondents reported a continuing effort to focus the curriculum on student personal development as well as academic achievement. One hundred percent of the respondents indicated that administrators and teachers collaborated in making the decisions that shaped school-wide policies affecting students.

Clearly, these data indicate that the schools in this national sample do report the inclusion of the central organizational components of the middle school philosophy, in spite of their diversity with grade levels included, size, location and other factors. They are alike organizationally, and that likeness reflects a commitment to the implementation of concepts at the heart of the middle school movement. There should no longer be much doubt about how important interdisciplinary team organization and the advisor-advisee programs are to the middle school concept; nor, if we can believe the trends which appear in the recent research, should we doubt that these programs make a positive difference in the lives of students. The remainder of the report of this survey will supply example after example of the ways in which these programs improve the education of young adolescents.

Student Achievement

The findings of this study dispute earlier opinions that academic achievement is either unaffected or only modestly improved by a move to middle school organization. Rather than the typical finding of no differences, sixty-two percent of the respondents in this study described consistent academic improvement. An additional twenty-eight percent of the respondents supplied specific results demonstrating increased scores on state assessment tests, the California Achievement Test, the Iowa Test of Basic Skills, and similar tests since their schools became middle schools. An overwhelming majority, eighty-five percent, observed that teacher confidence in student abilities had increased, which, many suggested, led to higher expectations and greater student productivity in academic classes. Other aspects of reorganized programs positively affecting student learning included coordination of skills and subjects by interdisciplinary teams as well as greater teacher awareness of preadolescent needs and abilities. Below is a small sample of the dozens of verbatim comments that indicate respondents' satisfaction with academic achievement and middle school organization.

After adopting the middle school philosophy, we found that our scores on the ITBS have been above grade level on Iowa norms approximately 90% of the time during the last 10 years.

Standardized test scores in the formative years of the middle schools, 1969-70, were in the 75% range nationally per grade. The 1983 scores for the total battery of the CAT were as follows: Grade 5-92%, Grade 6-82%, Grade 7-91%; and Grade 8-92%.

Teachers working on interdisciplinary teams realize more the importance of reinforcing skills and concepts in all subjects, not only in their specific content areas. The science teacher, for example, realizes his role in teaching not only science, but also reading, handwriting, vocabulary, etc.

Since students work at levels at which they can achieve, achievement is higher.

Innovative teaching strategies and grouping practices contribute to greater student achievement.

Team organization, more awareness of student levels, and more emphasis on the individual student lead to better achievement.

School Discipline

Reorganization improved school discipline in almost every measurable manner. Tardiness and truancy moderately or greatly decreased, according to a majority of respondents, as did school vandalism and theft. Approximately 80% noted a significant reduction in office referrals and suspensions, while close to 60% expelled fewer students after the transition. Almost 90% observed that teacher and staff confidence in managing disruptive students increased, diminishing administrative involvement in discipline in many schools. Reorganization to an exemplary middle school program clearly improves school and classroom discipline.

All of the anecdotal evidence supported the positive effects of middle school programs on school discipline. Specifically, interdisciplinary team organization and grouping students in houses enabled teachers to develop consistent procedures for handling disruptions, wrote one-fourth of the respondents. Advisor-advisee programs and greater emphasis on school guidance improved communication and empathy between teachers and students, often defusing volatile emotions before they exploded in classroom confrontations. The cultivation of parental support in enforcing disciplinary actions greatly improved student behavior. Implementing highly structured discipline plans, such as Glasser's Reality Therapy and Canter's Assertive Discipline, which need teacher-teacher and teacher-administrator collaboration in order to be fully effective, was facilitated by staff development programs accompanying reorganization. Several respondents suggested that moving ninth graders to high schools left a group of younger adolescents more similar developmentally and less sophisticated and troublesome in general. The following quotes represent perceptions held by administrators of the effects of reorganization on school discipline in the exemplary middle schools we surveyed:

School climate/behavior is much improved since the middle school was adopted. Relations between races improved. Discipline problems were not eliminated, but their severity diminished. Teachers became more attuned to causes of unacceptable behavior.

We saw an unbelievable reduction in discipline when the transition was made. Students now take pride in the fact that school discipline problems almost vanished.

We now have approximately one-half the number of referrals in comparison to the junior high.

The Advisory-Advisee program has enhanced a strong, positive relationship between teachers and students and increased peer tolerance of each other's personal problems. This understanding and interaction have induced self-discipline and a drastic decline in referrals for disciplinary problems. We have not had to suspend or expel anyone since the reorganization to middle school.

The counseling approach to discipline and thorough understanding of the child in the middle helped improve school-wide discipline. With the reorganization, ninth graders became a part of the high school. A particular set of behavior characteristics and influence of this age group was removed from the school, e.g. alcohol and drug abuse and distribution, intimidation, fighting, and theft. The team concept has made it easier for teachers to work with the administration, students, and parents in resolving discipline problems exhibited by 7th and 8th graders.

Student Personal Development

Certainly, one of the long-espoused goals of the middle school has been to focus on the unique nature and needs of younger adolescents. This study indicates that exemplary middle schools have been very successful in promoting student personal development. Student emotional health, creativity, and confidence in self-directed learning were positively affected by reorganization, testified over 80% of the respondents; better than 90% believed that student self-concept and social development benefited, too.

Anecdotal evidence overwhelmingly credited middle school programs with enhancing each student's personal and social skills. The success of team organization and teacher-based guidance in helping individuals develop closer peer relationships was cited repeatedly. Extracurricular and intramural athletic activities were designed to provide opportunities for all students instead of a precious few and invited greater student participation, interaction, and competition. Awards for leadership, good citizenship, and cooperation in and out of classes enabled those who weren't honor roll students or star athletes to experience the important satisfaction of recognition before peers. Interdisciplinary teams, classroom guidance, and exploratory programs increased opportunities for student involvement and accomplishments, significantly improving student personal development, according to respondents. A few observations selected from dozens supplied:

Teams stress the development of the whole student — social, emotional, physical, and intellectual...a strong team identity in each student promotes increased personal development.

Team structure allows more time and a friendlier organizational structure for personal development. Teachers have time to meet with and talk to students.

Students are assigned to teacher-advisors within the team. Teachers keep close contact with students and assist them with personal problems and social development.

Programs in our school which allow for personal development are intramural sports, non-competitive cheerleading, child-centered teams and special programs based on student choices.

Our school climate allows for recognition of individual growth.

Board participation in art, band, chorus, orchestra, a student aide program in the library, cafeteria, A-V room, and physical education classes, drama, newspaper, historical archives, horticultural society, interscholastic and intramural sports, archeological group, and community services contribute to personal development.

Reorganization was also identified as a chance to delay certain social pressures that seem to precipitate an undesirable sophistication in young people today. Schools can work with students before major growth spurts associated with puberty occur and can help them adjust to new academic environments before problems develop. "No school-sponsored dances certainly delays the mating process!" quipped one respondent. Others conveyed parental support for their efforts to slow down pre-adolescent maturation:

This is difficult to prove, but many students who have gone through the middle school program and are now at the high school report much easier adjustment and less stress with personal issues. Parents of our current students believe strongly that students are dealing with their personal development better because of middle school concepts, especially those parents of older children who went through the junior high school.

Our attempt was to delay the social pressures occurring in junior high school. To that end we have observed fewer socialization problems during our two years as a middle school. Surprisingly, we have had a strong vote of confidence from the parents.

We have won our parents over through the successes and happiness of their children.

Many comments specifically attributed gains in student personal development to effective teacher guidance. A part of the original junior high concept, the classroom advisory group is making a strong comeback in reorganized middle schools. Although many respondents indicated that it was difficult to implement successfully, they praised its impact on helping students understand themselves and others during the trying time of early adolescence. When conceived and conducted with care, advisor-advisee programs appear gratifying to all involved. A few supportive remarks follow:

Teacher-advisor programs started in 1975 to stress human development. Students are successful and happy with themselves. They take responsibility for their education.

The advisor-advisee home room was mixed equally with all grade levels, which gave fine leadership opportunities, good home room stability, and a vehicle from which the student council could operate successfully. Daily contact with the advisor is very productive.

We use the advisor-advisee program. We also have group counseling for kids in divorce situations, called KIDS, to help with personal development.

Small group guidance and instruction periods provide a setting and activities for students to clarify and to understand their own conflicts and stresses in society.

School Learning Climate

Recent studies analyzing school effectiveness correlate the atmosphere or learning climate with student behavior and achievement. Students who feel valued by teachers and who view school as more than just a place to meet friends tend to show respect for their schools in many ways. The exemplary middle schools in this study developed programs that demonstrate persistent caring for students as young people and create a school environment to meet their special academic and personal needs. Predictably, respondents supplied evidence indicating stronger school spirit since reorganization. Over ninety-five percent of them declared that student attitudes toward school and feelings about teachers were moderately or strongly positive, as a consequence of reorganization. Eighty-six percent witnessed greater student participation in special interest activities, while seventy-five percent noted better attendance at their middle schools.

Anecdotal descriptions of student enthusiasm for an involvement in school programs ran nearly five to one in favor of changes brought about by a move to middle school organization. Here are sample perceptions of school spirit and ways to develop it submitted by respondents:

Spirit is much improved. Activities such as Pride Week, Hat Day, Student Exchange Day, Spelling Bees, etc. develop team spirit which extends to the whole school.

Because between two-thirds and three-fourths of the students participate in clubs and athletics now, school spirit is tremendously increased. We eliminated cheerleaders, letter awards, cutting teams, etc. so that all who go out participate. Spirit is superb!

Emphasis has been placed on daily good citizenship awards, academic excellence, school skates, and after-school intra-murals. Students participate actively and strive to receive awards. We sell tee shirts and jackets with the school logo.

School spirit is visibly increased through posters, participation in contests, competitive activities between teams, etc. There is more pride demonstrated in spirit days and assembly behavior.

The 1,500 visitors to our school have always pointed to the positive atmosphere of our school, along with the students' pride in it, their work and their teachers. We do not have nor do we encourage typical junior-senior high type of activities.

In discussions of school district reorganization from junior high to middle schools, concern or fear that changing programs will diminish school spirit is often expressed. Educators and citizens argue heatedly about the proper role of interscholastic competition and accompanying functions like cheerleading and athletic awards. Proponents of such activities predict that eliminating them will negatively affect school spirit; opponents stress that their inclusion in schools means most students will be excluded from participating and recognition, weakening school spirit. The present survey indicates that when middle school curriculum is designed to encourage greater student involvement in different ways, removal or significant modification of interscholastic sports programs does not diminish student pride and positive feelings. Failure to compensate for altering conventional athletic competition during reorganization, however, can be costly to school pride.

The majority of respondents identified new activities that effectively replaced traditional ones in generating student excitement and participation. Advisory group and interdisciplinary team programs successfully stimulated students to get involved in their schools, as did offering intramurals, clubs, exploratory classes, and awards for effort and excellence. Several schools retained interscholastic sports and cheerleading by restructuring them to include more students or by shifting responsibility for them to community agencies allowed to use school facilities after hours. Representative comments below illustrate these alternatives:

> *School spirit is observed to be much better since the inclusion of a variety of exploratory activities, specifically: girls; extramural basketball, boys' extramural football, different intramural athletics, in-school practice for advanced band, prep band, jazz-rock ensemble, orchestra, string ensemble, mixed chorus, and 6th grade chorus. Providing learners with many opportunities to interact in both formal and informal settings appears to have increased student pride in our school.*

> *Good citizenship is appreciated as well as rewarded at our school. Each month approximately 45 students are recognized as "Students of the Month" for demonstrating outstanding citizenship and school spirit. Their names are announced over the intercom, they are given special certificates, and their pictures appear in the local paper.*

> *We dropped interscholastic athletics, but purchases of school yearbooks and jackets are up. There seems to be more pride in the wearing of school colors.*

> *In our school, students identify with their team and the school. Many teams have adopted mascots, slogans, and colors. Students participate more in school activities since the middle school began.*

> *The close student identification with their respective teams has promoted school spirit and inter-team competitiveness. In addition to participating in fund-raising, field trips, and our lunch time softball league, pupils direct their energies toward the culminating achievements that take place during the field day which is held the last week of school each year.*

> *Healthy school spirit competition is handled by grade levels competing against each other and other teams within a grade level. Teams select names, create banner flags displaying their colors. A lot of effort is made to reduce the "bigness" of the school to a small unit. Because all students are permitted to participate in the school athletic program, we found school spirit is very positive.*

Faculty Morale

Considering the complexities of educating American youth and frequent criticism by parents, politicians, and the press for not doing a satisfactory job, many public school teachers exhibit alarming but understandably low morale in and away from their classes. Not so in the nation's exemplary middle schools. An impressive ninety-four percent of the respondents described staff morale and rapport as moderately or strongly positive following reorganization. Based on formal and informal observations, ninety-three percent concluded that a move to middle school organization favorably influenced staff attitude toward change, and eighty-two percent noticed increased staff participation in special interest activities following the transition. Over one-half of the respondents cited lower teacher absenteeism and turnover as indications of high morale, noting teachers fought transfers to other schools. All anecdotal comments but one praised the benefits to morale of implementing middle school philosophy. Teachers voiced greater job satisfaction, worked more closely, and spent more leisure time together, said respondents, Some of their comments follow:

The faculty is developing into a cohesive unit. Mutual trust and genuine concern are quite evident.

A district survey was made by the teachers' association and their report to the school board was that morale at the middle school was the highest in the district.

Faculty morale is more cohesive than junior or senior high staff. We have more articulation.

Morale has been a very positive factor for the success of the school. More teacher dedication and professionalism is the direct result of reorganization.

Many older faculty members say they have had some of their best years since coming to the middle school.

The staff is becoming better and better at decision-making that leads to better programming with kids in mind — and then feeling good about the positive feedback coming from kids as a result.

Such positive faculty morale did not magically appear when the middle schools opened their doors. Some faculty members lacked enthusiasm for reorganization, refusing to cooperate with efforts to involve them in the planning process. A noticeable number of secondary-trained teachers thought the new expectations of them were unreasonable and resisted change. As they enjoyed increased support on teams and more control over learning time, however, many skeptical teachers developed an appreciation for the appropriateness of middle school programs. Even those disillusioned with district policies and budgets, by a national clamor for educational reform, or with contract negotiations, often admitted later that reorganizaton improved schooling and made their jobs more rewarding. One respondent's comment that it took ten years before his staff truly supported the middle school concept suggests that considerable patience may be a prerequisite for developing strong faculty morale. Other comments expressed concern about the life span of staff enthusiasm in middle schools, mentioning that some teachers could over-extend themselves and tire within a few years if precautions were not taken.

One particular middle school program component believed by respondents to contribute greatly to staff morale was the interdisciplinary team organization. Previously-isolated instructors became team members and developed the same sense of belonging and camaraderie they hoped to instill in their students. The flexibility in scheduling inherent to team responsibility for a common group of students occupying generally the same area provided teachers with many options for instruction. Sharing knowledge of students and subjects increased their confidence and consistency. As a respondent exclaimed, "Four heads are better than one!" Working on a team, especially with close friends, can be more difficult than working alone, warned another, although it can be well worth the effort. Below are other comments summarizing positive feelings about teams and faculty morale:

Teaming has provided a camaraderie that never existed in our junior high program. A new staff member arriving on the scene has immediate support from returning teachers both socially and professionally.

Every staff member belongs to a team and helps set team and professional growth goals each year. They also have opportunities to participate in team and building decision-making processes.

The teaming concept has improved morale among faculty members. Scheduled team planning time has enabled the staff to share ideas with each other, use each other as sounding boards, plan interdisciplinary units, and become more involved with the students and school. Grade level and entire faculty social events have helped also.

The key to middle schools is the interdisciplinary team. All other aspects depend on the fostering, nurturing, encouraging, and developing of strong teams.

Staff Development

Reorganization to middle schools, according to respondents, provided ample opportunities for teachers, principals, and district administrators to coordinate efforts to improve instruction and classroom management by implementing extensive staff development programs. Acknowledging that some teachers are more responsive to change than others and that occasionally staff members can be worn down by too much in-service training, the exemplary middle school administrators in this survey nonetheless noted greater staff involvement in designing and executing philosophy, curriculum, and objectives when they conducted staff development programs to facilitate reorganization. Inservice programs about characteristics of the age group, interdisciplinary teaming, and advisory/advisee groups, supplemented with educational programs applicable to all grades, such as Effective Schooling, Instruction Theory Into Practice, Assertive Discipline, and Reality Therapy, brought to the middle school staff research findings and practices that can revitalize teaching and learning in these crucial grades. Most schools assessed needs and interests of their teachers prior to, during, and after the transition, enlisted the aid of local universities and colleges when possible, encouraged individual and group attendance at state and national conferences about middle school education, and generally scheduled dozens of inservice sessions to improve instruction.

Teacher receptivity to staff development, characterized by greater participation in inservice education and favorable responses to surveys undertaken at different times during reorganization, was and continues to be positive, particularly when teachers are involved in the planning of the transition from the beginning. Respondents considered such teacher involvement crucial to establishing successful middle schools and indicated that teachers in the middle truly appreciated a concerted effort to develop an educational program specifically tailored to accommodate their students. Frequently, well-established middle school programs produce faculty members who serve willingly as resources for newly reorganized schools; teachers and administrators become consultants for other districts. If done well, moving to middle schools can be an excellent opportunity to implement effective staff development that involves and excites teachers who too often feel ignored and beleaguered. Below are samples of respondents' comments about the positive effects of reorganization on staff development:

Teachers have a part in planning staff development activities around their needs and interests. Many middle school teachers are consultants to other nearby districts for inservice education.

Staff was involved from day one. They wrote philosophy, objectives and curriculum.

An outstanding program was in effect during the planning stages. Program included school visitations and attendance at State and National symposiums.

We are constantly involved in staff development. Without this, the school would lose its effectiveness. We have six contract days for workshops, in-services, etc. We budget money to take team members out of the building, train them and they, in turn, are responsible for training the other staff members.

The third Monday of each month teachers participate in a staff development session. The topics a teacher may select range from characteristics of a M.S. child, effective teaching practices, learning styles, and "swap shop", all conducted by our staff.

Other schools are calling our staff to do in-service programs.

Parental Involvement and Support

Respondents to this survey proudly described the positive parental involvement and support they experienced after reorganization to middle schools. They cited better attendance at open houses, conferences, and PTA meetings as well as a greater propensity to volunteer as chaperones for field trips, dances, or other school socials. Parents offer to help in libraries, cafeterias, and classrooms, to coach intramural athletics, and to teach minicourses in many of the exemplary middle schools. Administrators in these schools cultivated parental involvement during all stages of the transition, anticipating the contributions and support that parents could give to the new program. They took pains to explain why and how reorganization would improve schooling for their children and established communication channels that encouraged parents to ask questions and to make suggestions at any point of the move to the middle school.

Observing that most parents welcomed invitations to become involved in their children's schools, they sought to capitalize on parental willingness to share responsibility for their children's education and were well-rewarded for their efforts. One respondent boasted that parents told him, "You cannot change your program until my last child has gone through it!" Another said, "My child likes school for the first time." Others noted that parents of their students rallied to prevent tampering with successful programs, such as team organization and small group advisory periods. Parents often voiced support for the middle school at board meetings and frequently voted to fund the money needed to maintain the level of educational services characteristics of exemplary middle schools. Like the majority of middle school teachers, middle school parents genuinely appreciate the attention focused on their children's learning and behavioral needs by conscientious reorganization and are eager to help middle schools meet these needs. Parental support for middle school programs is evident in the following quotes:

From 1969-72 the community was highly critical of the Middle School. Since the team organization and a true Middle School posture, the support has grown to where the parents feel we are the best school in town.

Our parent/school advisory council has been one of the factors in creative good participation among parents for the school — parents are involved in nearly every facet — the support has been increasing, and it has been good for the staff to feel it.

Very positive. Parents like what's happening, especially the genuine concern each team of teachers develops for the students.

Parent volunteers work in media center, clinic, serve lunch, act as classroom resources, teach English as a second language, and teach minicourses.

Excellent. It is felt that this is their school, and parents love meeting with their teachers. Chaperones and volunteer help have increased significantly.

Very positive feedback. We are getting students from private schools.

Community Involvement and Support/Media Coverage

Admitting that community concern for the cost of public education can spell financial trouble for school programs, particularly for reorganizational plans needing money to provide facilities and to retrain staff, our respondents nonetheless reported favorable community support. Businesses, civic organizations and community leaders resembled the parents in their willingness to contribute to the schooling of middle level students when invited to do so by administrators and teachers in exemplary middle schools. They both attended and presented assemblies, fund-raising events, and career awareness programs, generating and diffusing valuable support for the middle school throughout the community. People with and without children in the schools volunteer to cover classes, to tutor exceptional students, and to sponsor clubs, according to many administrators in our survey. "All we have to do is ask!" wrote one respondent of his community's eagerness to help in the school. Others related that although they would like to have even more community involvement and support, they were generally pleased with existing levels. Those who brought different elements of the community, such as a policemen, alcohol and drug abuse counselors, and public relations experts from businesses and corporations, into their schools as resources for the curriculum to promote civic awareness and responsibility noted definite improvements in student behavior and attitudes. The schools and surrounding communities benefited from such combined efforts to present a balanced program for students in middle grades. Support becomes mutual, sincere, and effective when nurtured during reorganization and carefully sustained afterwards.

Here are examples of responses that reveal community involvement and approval of exemplary middle school programs:

> *The President of our PTSA and three other officers do not have children in our school, but they are involved. About 60% of our two school communities do not have students in any school but support us in many ways — with time, energy, ideas and money.*

> *We have Grandparents Day, Rotary Day, Kiwanis Day, High-12 day, and many other "days" to get our non-parent population in our school. Great reaction to this program. The community passes our Bond issues.*

> *The community voted additional taxes to pay for the construction of the new buildings and pay for the new program. They have been very supportive.*

> *Through the Adopt-a-School, PALS, and Career Education program, 2876 hours of volunteer services were given to the students at our school in 1982-83. During the first three months of the year, our school had 40 volunteers working in the school. The Junior League and the Rotary Club in cooperation with the middle school staffs have initiated two programs for students and parents. One deals with substance abuse and the other with divorce.*

> *The school is actually a point of real pride. The Economic Development Council uses the school as one of their selling points. The community has a lot of knowledge about the school and supports the quality of education.*

Three-fourths of the respondents felt that newspaper, radio, and television coverage was positive during the reorganization, although a few wished it had been more in-depth and consistent. Districts employing professional public relations officers to convey school news to the media noticed greatly improved coverage; others were pleased that certain middle school components differing from traditional junior high programs, such as team organization and advisory efforts, caught reporters' eyes and were publicized, giving exemplary middle schools occasion to explain and to justify these differences. Many of the exemplary middle schools surveyed had received national recognition for excellence and enjoyed particularly favorable press, sometimes to the chagrin of other schools in the district or region. Most respondents hoped to improve media coverage of their programs by continuing to develop successful learning environments appropriate for their students. As one administrator quipped, "More students being recognized means more names in the paper, which sells more papers!"

One-fourth of the respondents lamented the lack of favorable press their school received during reorganization, stating that the media in their areas publicized conflicts between the school board and superintendent or shortcomings of the educational system more zealously than they praised instructional programs. Their comments suggested that sensationalism and criticism of local schools appeared to be more newsworthy and that having positive reports printed or telecast was difficult.

Many anecdotes describing media coverage, or the lack thereof, of the exemplary middle school were submitted. A few follow:

The district has a half time public relations person. Middle school staff initiate calls to press and create a feeling of openness. We thank the press when they deserve it.

Media will print stories when we want them to — very cooperative about printing meeting dates and stories about student projects — the school usually writes them or provides details for the story.

Local media coverage is very good when we devote time to pressuring the press.

Improvement has occurred after the initial year when many concerns surfaced and the community adjusted to the new elementary, middle school, and high school boundaries. A number of positive in-depth stories or features occur frequently. We had coverage of the Middle School Assessment recently completed.

Fair. We must send them all positive data. They look for us only if they hear of something negative or controversial. I guess this is what they believe news is.

Inadequate — they don't understand despite invitations to all meetings and many materials being sent to the educational writer.

We must constantly work on it to get anything positive about school in general.

High School Staff Perceptions

In stark contrast to the strong vote of confidence given to reorganization by middle school parents, teachers, and surrounding communities, support wavered among high school staff. Just over half of exemplary middle schools surveyed reported praise and approval from the upper grade teachers to whom they sent students. Most of these added that to earn such good marks, they had to overcome earlier suspicions and fears voiced by high school teachers doubting the seriousness of middle school programs. Many acknowledged district emphasis on K-12 curriculum and articulation as very helpful in establishing positive reputations and relations with high schools. A few noted that reorganization inspired some high school teachers to improve their programs by implementing ninth grade interdisciplinary teams and by maintaining the close parent-teacher-student contact developed in the middle grades. Respondents indicated great pride when told by senior high staff that the middle school years must be doing something right since students were well prepared for their final school years. Even this group enjoying favorable opinion from their secondary counterparts, however, express difficulty in pleasing high school personnel.

The other forty-six percent of the respondents reported criticism, fickle support, or apathy toward their programs. Often high school teachers said that middle schools were too elementary, that only they in the upper grades really teach, and that it would be a step down to teach in middle school. The absence of ability grouping and interscholastic athletics was thought to disrupt high school programs, eliciting more negative comments. If reorganization moved ninth graders to high schools, contributed to overcrowding, or required a greater budget than allotted to the high school, many instructors there were quick to disregard any merit assessed by a program based on preadolescent needs. Dissatisfaction in high school perceptions of middle schools was apparent, but many respondents suggested that schools at all levels should work hard to improve communication and cooperation. A few proposed re-assigning district teachers to different buildings and grades more often and encouraging K-12 articulation to promote positive feelings among schools:

Middle school success produces high school successes. Articulation is improved. Programs are continued from one level to another.

The HS principals indicate that the students from the middle schools adjusted better than the students before them. The students exhibit more self-discipline and are better prepared. One high school staff gave their feeder middle school a standing ovation.

Have slowly changed over the years. At the beginning they were negative toward the middle school, but as students moved into the high school and were more successful the attitudes began to change. At present we have a continuing dialogue with the high school staff.

Original high school staff misconceptions and poor attitudes have eroded as successes and staff accomplishments continue. A middle school assessment completed last year and reported to the Board in August showed inservice is needed for Elementary & HS to fully inform each of components and programs.

High school teachers who once taught in middle school or have shared teaching assignments in M.S. have very positive views of middle school. Those who have had no experience with this age group tend to think we should be more like a high school.

Still not as good as we would like. They still think of us as Jr. varsity teachers. They don't understand middle school children and how we have learned to educate them.

They think we baby them too much, although ''they'' say students are better disciplined, better behaved, and more goal oriented.

SUMMARY AND CONCLUSIONS

This study sought to provide additional data which can be brought to bear on two important questions pertaining to school district implementation of middle school programs. To what extent do middle schools identified as exemplary contain program components which conform to the recommendations of the literature on middle school education? If common program components exist in these reputedly successful middle schools, what have been the outcomes of the implementation of these components? An exceptionally high percentage of responses to the inquiry were received.

Results indicate that middle schools which manage to receive a reputation as highly successful as very similar in terms of the components of the program. The programs common to these exemplary middle schools do tend to conform to there recommendations in the literature of middle level education in the last half century. Such programs, too, are distinctly different from those common to elementary and high school. Furthermore, when implemented in this way, the results are dramatically positive. Academic achievement, student behavior, school learning climate, faculty morale, staff development, and a number of other factors are affected in positive ways.

The results of this study do not, of course, indicate that other programs for the organization and operation of middle level schools are necessarily less effective. These data do not tell us whether the results enjoyed by the schools in this study are or are not present in other middle schools which have not been designated as exemplary. A study of a similar sample of more conventional junior high schools identified as highly successful, or a sample of other middle schools which have not been so identified, might yield similar results. Other explanations, (e.g., a Hawthorne effect) might be responsible for the reported outcomes of the reorganization; or it may simply reflect a change to a less turbulent period in American education.

We can be more assured, however, of emerging answers to the questions which were the focus of this study. Good middle schools are very similar programatically, and they work extremely well.

Without claiming that the truth is finally known, it does seem possible to increase the level of confidence with which middle school educators discuss the efficacy of the programs they advocate. The evidence, meager though it may be at this point, indicates that restructuring the school organization provides new opportunities for teachers to work together in ways that focus on students as well as subject matter. This sharp focus on students may then create a milieu in which adults become more willing, because the students are more like real human beings to them, to adapt all of their school practices to the individual differences of the students. The new structure may contribute to the eagerness of teachers and students to work together to create more positive environments for learning and for personal development. Knowing their students more personally may make it possible for teachers to find more opportunities to reward and praise their students, to create situations in which the students can assume more responsibility and engage in greater degrees of participation in the life of the school.

It does seem possible now, at least tentatively, to say that it is not the name of the school or the grade levels that make the difference. It is not the physical facilities or the backgrounds of the teachers. It is the way in which people, adults and children, are organized to work and learn together. Perhaps curriculm changes and instructional improvements will be next.

REFERENCES

Alexander, W.M. & George, P.S. (1981). *The exemplary middle school.* New York: Holt, Rinehart and Winston.

Coleman, J. (1966). *Equality of educational opportunity.* Washington, DC: U.S. Government Printing Office.

Damico, S. (1982). The impact of school organization on interracial contact among students. *Journal of Educational Equity and Leadership,* 2, 238-52.

Doda, N.M. (1983, March). *Middle school organization and teacher world view.* Paper presented at the meeting of the American Educational Research Association, New York City.

Doda, N.M. (1984). Teacher perspectives and practices in two organizationally different middle schools (Doctoral dissertation, University of Florida, 1984). *Dissertation Abstracts International,* 45/10, 3058-A.

Dorman. G. (1983). Making schools work for young adolescents. *Educational Horizons.* 61, 175-82.

George, P. (1983). *The theory z school.* Columbus, OH: National Middle School Association.

George, P. (1975). *Ten years of open space schools: a review of the research.* Gainesville, FL: The Florida Educational Research and Development Council. *Research Bulletin.*

Johnston, J.H. (1984). A synthesis of research findings on middle level education. In J.H. Lounsbury (Ed.), *Perspectives: middle school education, 1964-1984.* Columbus, Ohio: National Middle School Association.

Klingele, W.E. (1985). Is the middle school just an educational fad? Concerns of a teacher educator. *Middle School Journal,* 16, (2), 14-15.

Levine, D.E. Levine, R.F., & Eubanks, E. (1984). Characteristics of effective inner-city intermediate schools. *Phi Delta Kappan,* 65, 707-11.

Lipsitz, J. (1984). *Successful schools for young adolescents.* New Brunswick, NJ: Transaction Books.

Lipsitz, J. (n.d.). *Successful schools for young adolescents: a summary.* Carrboro, NC: The Center for Early Adolescence.

McEwin, K.C. & Clay, R. (1983). *Middle level education in the United States: a national comparative study of practices and programs of middle and junior high schools.* Boone, NC: Appalachian State University.

National Institute for Education. (1983). *A study of the demography of schools for early adolescence.* January 1981. Washington, DC: U.S.D.O.E. Statistical Information Office.

Rutter, M., Maughan, B., Mortimore, P., Ouston, J., & Smith, A. (1979). *Fifteen thousand hours: secondary schools and their effects on children.* Cambridge, MA: Harvard University Press.

Wayson, W.W., DeVoss, G.G. Kaeser, S.C., Lasley, T., Pinnell, S.S., & the Phi Delta Kappa Commission on Discipline. (1982). *Handbook for developing schools with good discipline.* Bloomington, IN: Phi Delta Kappa.

Publications
NATIONAL MIDDLE SCHOOL ASSOCIATION

Treasure Chest, Cheryl Hoversten, Nancy Doda, John Lounsbury (268 pages)

Homework: A New Direction, Neila A. Connors (104 pages)

Professional Preparation and Certification, National Middle School Association (24 pages)

On Site: Preparing Middle Level Teachers Through Field Experiences, Deborah A. Butler, Mary A. Davies, and Thomas S. Dickinson (84 pages)

As I See It, John H. Lounsbury (112 pages)

The Team Process: A Handbook for Teachers, Third and enlarged edition, Elliot Y. Merenbloom (173 pages)

We Who Laugh, Last, Julia T. Thomason and Walt Grebing (64 pages)

Life Stories: The Struggle for Freedom and Equality in America, Lynn L. Mortensen, Editor (166 pages)

Education in the Middle Grades: Overview of National Practices and Trends, Joyce L. Epstein and Douglas J. Mac Iver (92 pages)

Middle Level Programs and Practices in the K-8 Elementary School: Report of a National Study, C. Kenneth McEwin and William M. Alexander (46 pages)

A Middle School Curriculum: From Rhetoric to Reality, James A. Beane (84 pages)

Visions of Teaching and Learning: Eighty Exemplary Middle Level Projects, John Arnold, Editor (160 pages)

The New American Family and the School, J. Howard Johnston (48 pages)

Who They Are, How We Teach: Early Adolescents and Their Teachers, C. Kenneth McEwin and Julia T. Thomason (26 pages)

The Japanese Junior High School: A View from the Inside, Paul S. George (56 pages)

Schools in the Middle: Status and Progress, William M. Alexander and C. Kenneth McEwin (112 pages)

A Journey Through Time: A Chronology of Middle Level Resources, Edward J. Lawton (36 pages)

Dynamite in the Classroom: A How-To Handbook for Teachers, Sandra L. Schurr (272 pages)

Developing Effective Middle Schools Through Faculty Participation, Second and enlarged Edition, Elliot Y. Merenbloom (122 pages)

Preparing to Teach in Middle Level Schools, William M. Alexander and C. Kenneth McEwin (64 pages)

Guidance in Middle Level Schools: Everyone's Responsibility, Claire Cole (31 pages)

Young Adolescent Development and School Practices: Promoting Harmony, John Van Hoose and David Strahan (68 pages)

When the Kids Come First: Enhancing Self-Esteem, James A. Beane and Richard P. Lipka (96 pages)

Interdisiciplinary Teaching: Why and How, Gordon F. Vars (56 pages)

Cognitive Matched Instruction in Action, Esther Fusco and Associates (36 pages)

The Middle School, Donald H. Eichhorn (128 pages)

Long-Term Teacher-Student Relationships: A Middle School Case Study, Paul George (30 pages)

Positive Discipline: A Pocketful of Ideas, William Purkey and David Strahan (56 pages)

Teachers as Inquirers: Strategies for Learning With and About Early Adolescents, Chris Stevenson (52 pages)

Adviser-Advisee Programs: Why, What, and How, Michael James (75 pages)

Evidence for the Middle School, Paul George and Lynn Oldaker (52 pages)

Involving Parents in Middle Level Education, John W. Myers (52 pages)

Perspectives: Middle Level Education, John H. Lounsbury, Editor (190 pages)

Teacher to Teacher, Nancy Doda (64 pages)

Early Adolescence: A Time of Change-Implications for Schools, Videocassette (37 minutes)

Early Adolescence: A Time of Change-Implications for Parents, Videocassette (50 minutes)

NATIONAL MIDDLE SCHOOL ASSOCIATION
4807 Evanswood Drive
Columbus, Ohio 43229-6292

(614) 848-8211
FAX (614) 848-4301